AIRFIELD F

PRESTWI

by Peter Berr

The first photograph of an aircraft at Monkton was recently found by aviation historian Tom MacFadyen. It shows Royal Flying Corps BE.2 273 and was taken on 25 July 1913, during Territorial Army manoeuvres at Gailes and along the Ayrshire Coast.

Twenty years later, in July 1933, De Havilland Fox Moth G-ACBZ of John Sword's Midland & Scottish Air Ferries landed in a field by the village of Monkton, just north of the seaside town of Prestwick, on the Ayrshire coast. At least two of Sword's Fox Moths, G-ACCB and 'CCT had been flown over from Renfrew Airport by pilots Winnifred Drinkwater and James 'Jimmy' Orrell as early as 16th April 1933 to conduct pleasure-flying. Sword lived at Craigwell in Ayr and asked an early Aerodrome Control Officer from Croydon, Jimmy Jeffs, to survey the area for a possible airfield. Jeffs selected a site west of the Ayr to Monkton road, opposite the entrance to Orangefield Mano

agreed that Sword's pilots could use the field and in 1934, Prestwick airfield appeared in the Air Pilot. That same year, DH84 Dragon airliners of Midland & Scottish were to be seen in 'The Meadow' alongside Orangefield, both in service and when a diversion from Renfrew airfield was necessary due to bad weather. A team from the RAF was also in the area at this time, surveying the Ayrshire coast for possible land and seaplane bases.

With the threat originating from German rearmament, the Government had decided in 1934 to increase the strength of the Royal Air Force from 41 to 128 first-line squadrons. To keep within the annual Treasury Budget, the Air Ministry offered RAF pilot-training contracts to private companies, who would fund the purchase of landing fields and aircraft and provide the training schools.

The log entry for Midland and Scottish Air Ferries DH83 Fox Moth G-ACCT dated 22.4.33 by pilot Jimmy Orrell showing an afternoon of pleasure-flying at Preswick. The aircraft was just over one month old.

(1) Journey from Renfrew (2) To Prestwick return

OPERATING CREW. (3) Names.	(4) Duties.	(5) Incidents and Observations.	VISA. (10) By the Aeronautical Authorities.	(11) By the Customs Authorities.
J H Orrell	Pilot.			

(6) Date.	(7) Places of Departure, of intermediate landings and of arrival.	Times. (8) Arrival.	(9) Departure.	
22.4.33	Renfrew	/	1400	
"	Prestwick	1420		
"	"		2000	
"	Renfrew	2015		
	Joyriding 1 hr. 5 mins			Total time – 1 hr. 40 mins.

(12) Signature of Officer in charge J H Orrell

The Commanding Officer of 602 (City of Glasgow) Squadron of the AuxAF, Flt. Lt. Douglas Hamilton, Marquis of Clydesdale, and his deputy, Flt. Lt. David McIntyre, had recently been the first pilots to fly over Mount Everest. Squadron pilots were well aware that when cloud or visibility conditions prohibited their landings at their base at Abbotsinch, near Glasgow, they only needed fly south-west to the Ayrshire coast, where it was always clear, and land alongside Orangefield Manor at Prestwick.

Hamilton and McIntyre were able to interest the de Havilland Aircraft Company in the formation of a flying school, and so on 9 August 1935 Scottish Aviation was incorporated. David McIntyre wished the Company to buy land in the Heathfield area of Prestwick, but the local Council objected as this was earmarked for future housing (which was still under construction in 2000!). The initial purchase was of 297 acres including the Aitkenbrae and Newdykes Farms as well as the Cornmill, also known as Powbank Mill. At first, 157 acres was used as the airfield, bounded by the Pow Burn the Monkton-Sandyford-Coylton Road and around Orangefield Manor, but 140 acres to the north of the road was allowed to remain in crop. In 1937/38, a further 48 acres of Orangefield Mains farmland was acquired, including the field adjacent to the Manor, which extended to the boundary wall of the Ayr to Glasgow road. To provide the site for Scottish Aviation factory buildings in 1938, the 140 acre field was taken over and a further 39 acres of farmland was purchased including the Orangefield Mains farmhouse and steading. A final purchase of ten acres in 1939, included the Church of Scotland Manse and Glebe Lands, brought the total airfield site to 395 acres. The Manse became flats for SAL employees.

Prestwick airfield opens

An Air Ministry contract for the training of Auxiliary Air Force pilots was signed on 14 October 1935. With 34 pupils, eight instructors and a fleet of sixteen Tiger Moths, 12 Elementary & Reserve Flying Training School (E&RFTS) began operations on 17 February 1936, when it was officially opened by the Marquis of Clydesdale. It was soon shown that a high level of flying training hours could be achieved, although flying training was forbidden during Church hours on Sunday mornings! By December 1936, 9000 flying training hours had been completed, three times the Ministry estimate.

The design of the first buildings at Prestwick was based on the de Havilland School at White Waltham. Completed in January 1936, they included the flying school, administrative building and 'watch tower', linked to the first 'Tiger' hangar. This hangar would be used in postwar years as the aero-engine overhaul facility. In 1937/38, the school building was enlarged and the Anson hangar and another watch tower was added to the administration building. Orangefield Mains farmhouse was converted to an engineering workshop in November 1938 and was still in use in 1998. A new hangar, known as No.1 Factory, was sited east of the farmhouse. This hangar, later known as the 'Fokker' hangar, allowed the acceptance of early Air Ministry modification contracts and remains to this day, housing the training aircraft of the British Aerospace Flying College. Early pupil pilots were accommodated in two large wooden dormitories sited behind Orangefield Manor, which served as their mess. These are the earliest buildings at Prestwick and still serve as a store.

To celebrate Empire Air Day, Prestwick enjoyed its first air display on 23 May 1936 and in 1937 12 E&RFTS began training pilots each weekend for the RAF Volunteer Reserve. Hawker Hart aircraft were added for advanced training and a total of 50,000 flying hours had been completed by December 1938.

Impressed by the training results at Prestwick,

Prestwick's control tower, flying school and 'Tiger' hangar circa 1936. Scottish Aviations DH82A Tiger Moths G-ADWD and 'WJ await their next pupils. G-ADWJ is still exant. [D. McIntyre]

The main entrance and gardens at Prestwick before 1939. [via author]

the Air Ministry requested the formation of a Navigation School, and on 15 August 1938 1 Civil Air Navigation School (1 CANS) began operations with Anson aircraft. Just before the outbreak of War, three Fokker four-engined airliners from KLM were added to the School. 12 E&RFTS was redesignated 12 EFTS on 3 September and 1 CANS became 1 Air Observer & Navigator School (1 AONS) on 1 November , with 24 Ansons and two of the Fokker airliners. 2 (Supplementary) School of Wireless Telegraphy, a non-flying unit, was opened at the airfield in September and by the end of the 1939, the training fleet of aircraft had reached 120. To aid the training of navigators, radio communication and direction-finding equipment was installed at Prestwick in the following year, which was to lead to an important development at the airfield. Scottish Aviation also managed 4 AONS at Dumfries and 35 EFTS and 10 CANS at its airfield at Grangemouth, which had opened as recently as 1 July 1939. This airfield continued in use during World War Two and was finally closed in June 1955. It was then enveloped by a large oil refinery. To enlarge the engineering capability at Prestwick, new buildings would be required and David McIntyre found the answer in relocating the great 'Palace of Engineering' building used at the Glasgow Exhibition in 1938. This was moved to Prestwick and was completed in September 1940, becoming No.3 Factory.

War service

On the outbreak of War in 1939, the flying instructors were mobilised and Gp. Capt. McIntyre became Officer Commanding RAF Prestwick. Sandyford Road was closed, permitting the joining of the two landing grounds together. With experience in maintaining the training fleet of Tiger Moth, Hart and Anson aircraft, Scottish Aviation sought more of this lucrative work. In early 1939, SAL received modification contracts from Rollasons on Wellesley bombers and work from Blackburn's on the Skua and Roc. SAL next made rudders for Hawker Harts and Hurricanes, completing 350 in the first year. The next project was to be the building of Westland Lysander aircraft under subcontract, but this was not confirmed. Although the Lysander contract was much reduced, the new factory facilities attracted the attention of the Civilian Repair Organisation (CRO), and so Prestwick became a primary site for the repair of Spitfires and Hurricanes, completing twelve per week.

Scottish Aviation was also the parent company to the CRO based at the LMS Railway Wagon Works at nearby Barassie. Towards the end of 1940, the paint shop at Barassie was rearranged for the repair of damaged Spitfires. Rolls-Royce Merlin engines were removed and sent away for servicing and a roadway was laid across the railway tracks to a take-off strip laid out on an adjacent golf fairway. Selected staff were sent to Derby for training in aircraft repair and carpenters from the St. Rollox Carriage Works in Glasgow were also drafted in. The first aircraft was completed on 10 October 1941 and was towed across the railway. With only a small amount of fuel, it was flown from the fairway to Ayr (Heathfield) airfield, where flight tests were carried out.

Initially, the paint shop could accommodate twelve airframes, and this output was reached in February 1942. To increase working space, two Super Robin hangars were erected adjacent to the fairway for the final assembly of Spitfires and refitting of engines. They were in use by December 1942, by which time the work force totalled 240 males and 270 females. The paint shop could now house 25 fuselages and 25 pairs of wings under repair, with ten aircraft in the hangars for final assembly. By the end of the War, 1200 Spitfires had been refurbished at Prestwick and the Barassie Wagon Works.

Scottish Aviation acquired an old warehouse at 39, West Campbell Street in Glasgow, where the construction of de Havilland Queen Bee radio-controlled target aircraft (a pilotless version of the Tiger Moth) was sub-contracted to Messrs Morris and the West of Scotland Furniture Company. In August 1943 the first of a contract for 150 aircraft was completed, but in November the

Tiger Moths of 12 EFTS at Prestwick in 1939 [C. A. Nepean-Bishop via author]

number was reduced to 60, and the last Queen Bee was completed and test flown at Prestwick in December 1943. After completion they were transported to Prestwick, assembled and test flown before being delivered to Manorbier in Pembrokeshire.

To reduce the exposure of aircraft factories to enemy attack in the South of England, Saunders-Roe looked for a site along the Clyde for the maintenance of Catalina and Sunderland flying-boats. Following discussion with Saunders-Roe and the Minister of Aircraft Production, Lord Beaverbrook, Caird's Shipyard in Greenock was requisitioned on 10 June 1940 and Scottish Aviation was awarded a repair and overhaul contract. A supplementary site was developed at Largs, and many Catalinas for the RAF were delivered to this site. During the summer of 1944 and 1945, regular PB2Y-3B Coronado flying-boat services from Montreal/Boucherville, via Gander Lake, terminated at Largs.

Contracts and arrivals

A further contract came in July 1940, when Scottish Aviation was instructed to assemble sixteen American-built aircraft that had arrived at Glasgow, by sea. This led to the later assembly of numbers of Tomahawks, Mohawks, Kittyhawks, Martlets and Kingfishers, many of them at Abbotsinch and Renfrew airfields. The late Chief Test Pilot at Prestwick, Wg. Cdr. N. J. Capper, related how he flight tested all these types of aircraft. Aircraft maintenance work had been inspected by the Ministry of Aircraft Production until March 1942, when the MAP approved the Design Organisation of SAL to inspect their own work. In December that year, Douglas McIntyre visited Consolidated in California, manufacturers of the Catalina and Liberator and gained approval for SAL to modify their products to bring them up to British operational standards.

During the Norwegian campaign in the spring of

Fokker F.XXXVI G–AFZR, the former KLM PH-AJA 'Arend' was obtained by Scottish Aviation in 1939. It was used by 12 EFTS and 1 AONS after being impressed into the RAF in 1939. On 21 May 1940 it lost power on take-off at Prestwick, overshot and was damaged beyond repair. The serial number allocated to it, HM161, was never carried [C. A. Nepean-Bishop via author]

Among the Ansons operated by 1 Civil Air Navigation School at Prestwick in 1938 was N4922. Behind it are the original airport buildings [D. McIntyre/C. A. Nepean–Bishop via AJJ and author]

1940, Prestwick saw the transit movements of many military aircraft in support of this ill-fated campaign.

To provide fighter defence against air raids on industrial targets in Glasgow, a number of RAF squadrons from Fighter Command were based at Prestwick during 1940, including 141, 253, 602, 603, 610 and 615 Squadrons. During six weeks in September and October 1940, Bomber Command loaned 102 Squadron of Whitleys to Coastal Command for convoy escort duties, operating out of Prestwick.

In September 1940, 4 Ferry Pool of the Air Transport Auxiliary (ATA) moved into its headquarters, a derelict single-deck bus body parked on the north side of the airfield. This unit's task was to ferry aircraft to and from Maintenance Units throughout the UK. At nearby Heathfield, the site was acquired by the Air Ministry for a three-runway airfield for RAF Fighter Command, later named Ayr.

An Aircraft Interception/Air-Surface Vessel (AI/ASV) Radar School was formed at Prestwick in October 1940, with six Blenheim aircraft. This Unit was redesignated 3 Radio School on 27 December 1940.

The prewar Scottish Aviation 'watch office' on the north side of Prestwick airfield was initially used by the RAF Duty Pilot. In October 1940, an approach control facility was established in the Powbank Mill at Prestwick, with communications radio, an HF D/F station and a Radio Track Guide.

Transatlantic deliveries

The next event in the history of Prestwick was to have a far-reaching effect. Conscious of the threat of German U-boats to sea-borne food, oil, aircraft and war supplies across the north Atlantic Ocean, Prime Minister Churchill gave high priority to the formation of fifteen squadrons of RAF Coastal Command. To equip these squadrons, Lord Beaverbrook proposed to deliver by air the urgently needed Hudsons. The urgency of the situation may be judged from the 'Instruction to Proceed'. BOAC Captain D. C. T. Bennett was called before the Minister, who asked *"Can you air ferry 'planes from Canada to Britain?" "Yes"* replied Bennett. *"Right, off you go"* instructed the Minister. The risk of ferrying military aircraft by air across the Atlantic was considered acceptable, as this would reduce the transit time from four months to ten days, save shipping space and avoid losses to U-boats. In the event only a small number of losses were experienced by the British Air Ferry during the five long years of War.

With the establishment of Atlantic Ferry Organisation (ATFERO) headquarters at St. Hubert in Montreal and the completion of airfield facilities at Gander in October, it was now possible to despatch aircraft across the North Atlantic to Aldergrove in Northern Ireland. To ensure the safe navigation of these aircraft across the ocean, it was decided to fly aircraft in groups with a BOAC navigating pilot in command. The first Hudson arrived at Gander on 28 October 1940 and the first group of seven Hudsons, led by Captain Bennett, left there on 9 November and arrived safely at Aldergrove next day after a flight of eleven hours.

The exercise was repeated on 28/29 November, led by Captain Humphery-Page and again on 17/18 December, led by Captain Store. Due to weather conditions, one Hudson from each of these formations became separated, but using the radio direction-finding station at Prestwick, arrived overhead the airfield, circled and landed. Aircraft engineer Matt Dryden was sent out on his bicycle to see what this aircraft was. He remembers the rather scruffy-looking crew in civilian clothes who he took to the watch office to 'book in'. *"What is it and where are you from?"* enquired the Duty

Hudson T9465 The Spirit of Lockheed-Vega Employees had been paid for by the work-force and was delivered to the RAF via Prestwick. Later it served with 269 Squadron at Wick [via author]

Pilot. *"One Hudson, T9426, on delivery to the RAF..."* replied the Captain. *"...We left Gander just over ten hours ago"*. The Duty Pilot entered the details in his log, with the names of the crew, Captain Pat Eves, First Officer Donald Anderson and Radio Officer Godfrey. There was a silence before it was realised that this crew had just flown their new Hudson aircraft across the North Atlantic. It later transpired that Eves had left some golf clubs at Prestwick and Anderson's wife lived in Crieff! This scenario was repeated, with the next formation of Hudsons from Gander, when Captain Stafford arrived at Prestwick on 17 December in T9440.

The last formation of four Hudsons to Aldergrove was led by Captain Bennett, arriving there on 29 December. Thereafter single flights were made, due to the time taken to assemble a formation and once airborne, the stress of flying in formation in cloud, at night and in poor weather conditions. There was also the problem of the slow return sea passage for ferry crews. Most significantly, the destination was changed to Prestwick, due to its fine weather record and proximity to the preferred North Atlantic air routes. The first scheduled Gander-Prestwick Hudson flights, which landed on 11 February 1941, was made by Captain Allen in T9464.

Transatlantic terminal and control

From January 1941, the attic of the Powbank Mill on the edge of Prestwick airfield had been used as a temporary Fighter Command Ops Room under the Turnhouse Sector. On 4 April 1941 it was relocated in Rosemount House, on the Kilmarnock road. Transatlantic Air Control (TAC) Centre was formed on 15 August 1941 and joined the Approach Control Unit in Powbank Mill, providing a local control service until permanent quarters were completed at nearby Redbrae House.

On 2 July 1941 Prestwick was requisitioned and was transferred from Scottish Aviation to the Air Ministry. RAF Prestwick came under Technical Training Command, which was also responsible for the operation of 1 AONS, 12 EFTS and 3 Radio School, which flew Botha aircraft. On 19 July 1941 all initial flying training ceased at Prestwick and moved to Canada under the Empire Air Training Scheme. Prestwick had already trained 1334 pilots, 1994 air observers and 1200 wireless operators.

TAC moved into the House on 6 November 1941 and at 1500 hours assumed Master Control of North Atlantic, Bermuda, Iceland and Russian flights, east of 30° West and north of 52°30'N. Overseas Air Control (OAC) at 44 Group Gloucester retained control of aircraft south of 52°30'N for flights from the UK to Gibraltar, Malta, North

Africa and the Middle East. The Oceanic Area Control Centre remained at Redbrae House until April 1972.

Following a disastrous fire on 3 February 1941, which gutted the prewar flying training administration offices and watch office at Prestwick, SAL took over a wing in Orangefield House on the south side of the airfield for the Company offices. A 'temporary' control tower was then built on top of the pitched roof of the House, which with its annexe was then requisitioned for war service by Scottish Aviation on behalf of the Ministry of Aircraft Production.

To accept the increasing number of aircraft expected to arrive at Prestwick from North America, a Civilian Reception Party was formed by Scottish Aviation in November 1940, to cater for the welcome, feeding and accommodation of crew and passengers in Orangefield House. With Sqn. Ldr. Jimmy Jeffs in charge, it became the major terminal in Great Britain for transatlantic arrivals and departures. An RAF Transatlantic Reception and Dispatch Unit (TRDU) then took over the duties of the Civilian Reception Party. The reception desk was in the Orangefield terminal and overnight accommodation for up to 139 persons was arranged in the nearby Towans and Auchencoyle Hotels, as well as in the 30 bedrooms in the annexe building. During the war, more than 500,000 people signed the sixteen visitor books in the Terminal.

Prestwick was still a grass airfield, but with the increasing number of Hudson, Fortress and Liberator aircraft expected to arrive, use of the newly-completed runways at nearby Ayr/Heathfield airfield sometimes had to be made. With Hudson flights across the Atlantic becoming routine, the first of twenty B-17C Flying Fortress I bombers (AN518-537) arrived at Gander in March 1941 to make the transatlantic crossing. AN534 left Gander on 13 April and arrived at Ayr after a flight of eight hours 49 minutes. More aircraft were flown across during the next two months, arriving at Prestwick or Ayr, but one landing was made at Squire's Gate (Blackpool) and one at Leuchars on the east coast of Scotland. The last of the twenty Fortresses (AN518) landed at Prestwick on 14 June.

A long, wide, paved runway was planned for Prestwick, suitable for all types of aircraft, and over the objections of some government officials, work began on a 6600 ft by 300 ft runway in March 1941. This, runway 14/32, was completed on 21 September, 1941 and a second, cross-wind runway 08/26 (4,500 feet x 300 feet), came into service in March 1942.

Return Ferry Service

The return of air ferry pilots to North America to collect more aircraft had been taking up to six weeks by sea, so to speed this, a Return Ferry Service was begun between Prestwick and Montreal, via Gander. Early production Convair LB-30 Liberator bombers were used, of which the first six LB-30A/YB-24 aircraft off the production line (AM258-263) were accepted in December 1940. Although having a long range, but lacking self-sealing fuel tanks and turbo-superchargers, these aircraft were modified in Montreal before joining the North Atlantic Return Ferry Service (RFS). Between March and June 1941, an additional nineteen LB-30B Liberators Mk.1 (AM910-929) were flown to Great Britain, to be immediately modified by Scottish Aviation at Prestwick for RAF Coastal Command and the Return Ferry Service. The first of these Liberators arrived at Squires Gate on April 9 (AM910) and the last (AM929) landed at Ayr on 20 August. Three were added to the Return Ferry Service, with a wooden floor over the bomb-bay and an oxygen system with up to twenty masks for passengers.

RFS Liberators were flown by BOAC crews, including Captains Wilcockson, Pearcy and O. P. Jones. The first Eastbound RFS Liberator flight (AM259), left Gander and arrived at Squires Gate on 14 March 1941 after a flight of

Boeing B-17C AN531 (formerly 40-2076) undertaking a proving flight from Boeing Field, Seattle before crossing the USA and the Atlantic, arriving in the UK at Preswick [Boeing]

A Liberator transport aircraft as used by ATFERO for returning ferry crews to Canada [P. M. Bowers via author]

nine hours and one minute. A second RFS Liberator (AM260) arrived at Squires Gate on 6 April. On 22 April Liberator AM912, (call-sign 9APW), flown by Captain Messenger, carried Brig. Worthington, Maj. Morres, Capt. Loomis and A.H.R. Smith from Gander, landing at Prestwick the following day. It then continued to the A&AEE at Boscombe Down for handling tests. After a delay caused by slight damage by an enemy raider on the night of 1/2 May, the first RFS westbound flight was made on 4/5 May by Capt. Youell in AM260, leaving Squire's Gate with seven ferry crew members on board. That same day, Liberator AM258 (9APB), flown by Capt. Bennett, arrived at Prestwick from Montreal and Gander after a flight of nineteen hours five minutes, with four passengers on board, including Air Marshall Sir Hugh Dowding. From July 1941, regular RFS services were flown six days per week and from 24 September the RFS was operated by BOAC under the AOC RAF Ferry Command.

The United States arrives

A North Atlantic service was begun by U.S. Army Air Corps Ferry Command (ACFC), on 1 July 1941. Using YB-24 Liberator 40-702 (call-sign MD120) flown by Lt. Col. Caleb V. Haynes, the flight left Washington for Ayr. Staging via Montreal, Gander and Reykjavik, it arrived on 3 July with personnel to assess the requirements for this air route. The return flight was made on 8 July, with a stop at Montreal, arriving back in Washington two days later. Twenty return flights were made on this 'Arnold Line' route, named after Col. William W. Arnold of Ferrying Command, before winter conditions suspended operations on 18 October. In addition to the YB-24, B-24A 40-2369 and 40-2371 to -2376 were flown. Two USAAF B-24A transports (40-2371/5), flown by Col. A. J. Harvey and Lt. Col. L. T. Reichers, staged through Prestwick from Washington in September 1941, carrying members of the Harriman Mission to Moscow. Even before the American entry into the war, a Detachment Eastern Terminus of the North Atlantic Division, US Army Air Corps, was established at Prestwick on 1 October 1941, staffed by military 'observers' and commanded by Maj. J. P. T. Hills.

Prestwick was now home to TAC, the Return Ferry Service, the 'Arnold' USAAC B-24 Liberator service, 4 Ferry Pilot Pool of the ATA, 3 Radio School and the Reception Unit of RAF Ferry Command. 1527 Blind Approach Training Flight was formed at Prestwick on 29 October 1941 with Oxford and Hudson aircraft, and next day 1425 (Communication) Flight was formed with Liberators to develop long-range ferry services to the Middle East. 3 Radio School was redesignated 3 Radio Direction Finding School in August 1942, but soon moved, taking twenty Botha aircraft to Hooton Park on 1 December.

Contract carriers

To provide overseas transport services, the US Government had designated several airlines as 'Contract Carriers', including American, American Export, Pan American and Trans World Airlines. TWA were the first to open a transatlantic service from Washington to

Prestwick, when Boeing 307 Stratoliner NC19908 *Apache* arrived from Reykjavik on 18 April 1942. B307s served the route well, making more than 120 crossings until replaced by C-54s on 16 November. The first transatlantic flight by a C-47 (41-7833), via Greenland and Iceland (the northern route), arrived at Stornoway on 3 July 1942 to deliver a low-frequency Radio Range station before continuing to Prestwick. On 28 August the Radio Range station at Prestwick became operational, completing the Army Air Corps Communication Service (AACS) 'airway' along the northern route, as comprehensive as could be found in the United States. The AACS established a code room and message centre with point-to-point, air/ground, navigation and joint tower control facilities at Prestwick on 1 July 1942. Two weeks later the first land-lines were operational with the British and with the HQ 1st Service Area at USAAF Station 597, Langford Lodge in Northern Ireland, later Base Air Depot 3.

'Bolero'

With bases and facilities ready, a major North Atlantic ferry operation took place when Project 'Bolero' was mounted. Between 23 June and 26 July 1942, 49 B-17Es of the 97th Bomb Group, 80 P-38F of the 1st Fighter Group and 52 C-47s of the 60th Troop Carrier Group were despatched to the 8th Air Force in England from Presque Island, Maine via the northern route to Prestwick, flown by their combat crews and escorted by B-17 navigation aircraft. Five B-17s and six P-38s were lost on the Greenland icecap during the operation, but their crews were saved. Several of the losses were believed to be due to radio bearing interference from a German submarine. The first combat B-17E to land at Prestwick, on 1 July, was 41-9085 *Jarring Jenny*. A second ferry operation, in July 1942, quickly followed the first, under the control of Air Transport Command. Lockheed P-38s from the 14th Fighter Group were escorted by B-17s from the 92nd and 301st Bombardment Groups across the North Atlantic without loss, together with C-47s of the 64th Troop Carrier Group. Additional Groups and replacement aircraft for the Eighth and Twelve Air Forces followed during the remainder of the year, the 2nd Ferrying Group delivering P-38 fighters. The first of these flights were six P-38Gs accompanied by a B-24D 'mother-ship' (41-11874). They left New Castle AFB on 5 September, routing Presque Isle, Goose, Bluie West 1 and Reykjavik, and all arrived at Prestwick on 16 September. The first direct Gander to Prestwick flight by sixteen USAAF B-17 Fortress bombers arrived at Prestwick on 6 September 1942 and the first formation flight of B-24D Liberators of the 93rd Bombardment Group flew in later that month.

Air Transport Command

The first Air Transport Command unit established at Prestwick was the 31st Ferrying Squadron, made up of men from the 10th AAF, the 2nd Communication Squadron and the 15th Air Corps Ferrying Squadron. On 7 September 1942, the 53rd Ferrying Squadron was formed at Presque Isle, becoming part of the 8th Ferrying Group, North Atlantic Wing, ATC. An HQ Squadron, USAAF ATC, was activated at Prestwick and on 1 April 1943 the 8th AFSC and HQ ATC were moved into the second floor of nearby Adamton House, assuming command of all USAAF personnel at Prestwick. 1403 Base Unit was activated on 24 September, with accommodation in Westburn House, adjacent to Redbrae, when all USAAF units at Prestwick were brought under the control of Station 3, ATC. To accommodate the increasing oceanic control operations at the airfield, US Army engineers erected six Seco-type huts around the Redbrae control building on 2 April 1943, and these huts continued to house the Oceanic Control Centre until 1972 and the later Scottish Airways Control Centre until demolished, with Redbrae House in 1978.

New Orangefield tower

To enlarge the terminal aircraft control accommodation at the airfield, the civil engineering division of Scottish Aviation was tasked with constructing a modern control tower on the pitched roof of the Orangefield terminal, and it was opened for operations on 13 December 1943. Immediately below the Tower was the RAF/USAAF W/T communication centre, together with MF and HF bearing and fixing aids. A new Long Range Cathode Ray (LRCR) direction-finding aid came into service, with stations in Iceland, Northern Ireland, Britain and the Azores.

1680 Flight

To continue the function of wartime air transport to the Western Isles, 1680 Flight had been formed at Abbotsinch in May 1943. The Flight moved to Prestwick in March 1944 and continued service with a variety of transport types, including Dominie, Anson, Dakota and Fokker F.XXII, until disbanding in February 1946.

RAF Reception Party

The RAF Trans Atlantic Reception Party, which had provided service to 2662 flights staging through Prestwick, was redesignated the Air Dispatch and Reception Unit in 1944. A total of 15,000 transatlantic aircraft had been controlled by the TAC Centre at Prestwick by 22 May that year. Prestwick tower recorded 7668 take-offs and landings in July 1944 and 7847 in August. To provide final approach guidance in bad weather at Prestwick, 3000 yards of sodium centre-line lights were laid right from the beach to Runway 14 threshold.

By 7 September 1944, BOAC had flown 1000 Return Ferry Service flights in their fleet of LB30/B-24 Liberators. 25,000 wartime transatlantic crossings had been completed by November, including transport and USAAF and RAF delivery flights. In all, 8400 aircraft had been delivered to the USAAF in Europe in 1944, including 6691 by air. Deliveries to the RAF totalled 1955 in 1944.

Transatlantic Air Control, 1940-45

Allied efforts in establishing transatlantic routes and services resulted in 38,044 crossings being controlled by the Prestwick TAC to 31 December 1945:

1940 :	26
1941 :	805
1942 :	2436
1943 :	6817
1944 :	16,224
1945 :	11,736
RAF Deliveries to the UK	5,793
Transport and Weather flights	15,808
USAAF deliveries	15,041
USN flights	731
RCAF flights	386
Miscellaneous	67

In addition, there at least 258 losses of transport and combat aircraft were recorded by the RAF Control Centres during transatlantic flights in World War Two. By November 1946, the BOAC Return Ferry Service had completed 2392 crossings of the North Atlantic, carrying some 22,500 passengers, 3.5m pounds of mail and urgent military supplies.

Foreign airlines

Using Lancastrian conversions, Trans Canada Airlines began a transatlantic service from Montreal to Prestwick on 1/2 July 1943. The Swedish Company ABA opened a Stockholm to Prestwick service with impressed B-17 Fortress transports on 9 October, 1944, completing eight return flights. The service continued in 1945 and had completed 31 return flights to 9 May. A stop was then added at Gothenburg and a weekday service continued from 21 May to 2 July, after which the service was routed to Croydon Airport.

At this time, several schemes were proposed by SAL and other interested bodies for the development of Prestwick as a post-War, transatlantic airport. These plans included new long runways and a flying-boat base adjacent to the airport.

Military run-down

The 1403 Base Unit USAAF at Prestwick had been reduced to a skeleton of personnel by October 1945 and Prestwick ceased to be a terminal for the US Air Transport Command. On 7 October, RAF Transport Command took control of the TAC service and at the end of November 1945 the USAAF returned the Operations Room and accommodation to the RAF. Orangefield Hotel became the civil passenger terminal, operated by Scottish Aviation.

Postwar developments

A compulsory acquisition order for the Prestwick site was served by the Ministry of Aviation on 1 April 1946, and Prestwick was designated the second international airport to London's recently opened Heathrow. The MCA also took over the airport hotel and handling services from Scottish Aviation. The Royal Air Force handed the tower, Approach Control and Transatlantic Air Control to

This view of the north dispersal in 1944, with a host of B–17s, Liberators for RAF Coastal Command, Dakotas, a Warwick, a B–25 and a C–54 in evidence, epitomises Prestwick's wartime function as a staging transatlantic staging post [G. L. R. Macadie]

the Ministry of Civil Aviation on 1 May and TAC became the Oceanic Area Control Centre (OACC) at Prestwick. Together with Shannon, 'Shanwick' was responsible for coordinating ATC clearances to departing and arriving flights through their national airspace, terminating at 30 degrees west. En-route re-clearances again involved co-ordination between each Centre. The introduction of these operating procedures was delayed until 1 November 1946.

From 9 April to 24 June 1945, Scottish Airways Ltd., under charter to Railway Air Services, operated a daily weekday service from Croydon to Prestwick, with a refuelling stop at Liverpool, using DH.89 Rapide aircraft.

The sudden ending of the war with Japan in August 1945 released some twenty C-54/DC-4 transports to Pan American, TWA and American Overseas Airlines for the start of commercial transatlantic services. An AOA DC-4, NX90901, landed at Prestwick on a proving flight on 22 September 1945, followed by NC90902 in October. Scheduled transatlantic commercial flights began through Prestwick on 21 May 1946, when a KLM DC-4 arrived from Amsterdam on its way to New York.

Scottish Airlines was formed on 1 January 1946 and began a return Prestwick to Belfast (Sydenham) service with DC-3s on 28 January under charter to BEA. From 16 September, the evening flights were to Aldergrove, as there was no night flying equipment at Sydenham. Scottish Airlines converted three Liberators to 24/30-seat transports and transatlantic survey flights were made to San Diego and Chicago. These flights led to the airline gaining charters with Liberators to North America, the Middle East, South Africa and within Europe. The airline began a service from Reykjavik to Copenhagen via Prestwick on 27 May 1946, under charter to Iceland Airways, Ltd, using Liberators, continuing with DC-3s for the Prestwick to Copenhagen sector. In their first year of operation, they carried 2912 passengers, 16,000 lbs of cargo and 26,500 lbs of mail, the route then being flown by Liberators. From 14 June, SAL began a freight service with Liberators to New York via Gander and Air France operated a three times weekly service to Paris using DC-3s. A service was also begun from Prestwick to Vaago in the Faroe Islands. On 10 April 1948, Iceland Airways took over the Iceland service with a single DC-4.

Nationalisation of air services

The nationalisation of British scheduled air services on 1 August 1946 saw Scottish Airlines flying return services for BEA from Renfrew and Prestwick to London, London to Aberdeen, Renfrew and Prestwick to Belfast with DC-3s. During the summer, charters were flown from Prestwick, Manchester and Liverpool to the Isle of Man. From 1946 for a couple of years, Air France too operated a three-times weekly service from Prestwick to Paris first with DC-3s and later with Languedoc transports.

In June 1947, the Scottish Airlines fleet included the five Liberators, thirteen DC-3s and one Fokker F.XXII, with Airspeed Oxford for instrument flying training. These services for BEA terminated in July 1947. In September, Scottish Airlines opened a twice-weekly charter service from Prestwick to Brussels and Manchester for COBETA. By the year end, Scottish

A fine picture of Dakota G–AGWS of Scottish Airlines parked in front of the Orangefield Hotel terminal building at Prestwick in 1946 [via author]

Civilianised Oxford G–AHDZ of Scottish Aviation parked in front of the Orangefield terminal building in about 1947 [P. H. T. Green collection]

Airlines had a fleet of 20 aircraft, 85 aircrew and had carried 43,702 passengers, 163,500 lbs cargo and 36,000 lbs of mail. But charters were slowly reducing, and Scottish Airlines turned to Luxembourg to assist the start-up of their own airline. They also took a 40% interest in Hellenic Airlines with a twice-weekly service from Prestwick to Tel Aviv, via London, Paris, Athens and Nicosia, using Liberators. The scheduled Prestwick to the Isle of Man service continued with Rapides or DC-3s. The aircraft fleet at November 1949, was five DC-3s, four Liberators and the Rapide.

Wartime services from Montreal to Prestwick, operated for the Canadian Government by Trans Canada Airlines, continued in their own name from 9 July 1946, still using Lancastrians, and the route was extended to London on 15 September. From 11 September, the Wednesday BOAC Constellation service from London to New York, was routed via Prestwick and Gander. The first non-stop New York to Prestwick flight was made on 6 December by BOAC Constellation Balmoral in eleven hours two minutes. Several medical flights had also been reported by BOAC, between Prestwick and Switzerland, with patients who had contracted TB. SILA was given permission from 16 September 1946 to stage their DC-4s through Prestwick on its Stavanger/Copenhagen-Gander-New York service. The BOAC Liberator Return Ferry Service to Montreal continued to pass through Prestwick.

Trans Canada replaced its Lancastrians with Douglas DC-4Ms on its service from Montreal to London via Prestwick on 14/15 April 1947. KLM replaced SAL on the Prestwick to Amsterdam route in April, extending the route to New York in May. Sadly KLM was to loose one of it's new Lockheed Constellations at Prestwick, when on 20 October 1948, PH-TEN *'Nijmegen'* under the command of their Chief Pilot Capt. Dirk Parmentier flew into power cables just over three miles east of the airfield in thick fog whilst attempting to land on Runway 26. All 40 people on board lost their lives. Parmentier has achieved worldwide fame in 1934 when his flew the KLM DC-2 from Mildenhall to Australia to win the Handicap section of the MacRobertson Air Race.

Scottish Airlines continued to offer charter services from Prestwick and American Overseas Airlines (AOA) commenced a twice-weekly service through Prestwick on 1 June, from New York and Reykjavik to Oslo or Stockholm and Helsinki with DC-4s, soon replacing them with Constellations.

American surplus Ground Controlled Approach (GCA) units were acquired by the MCA, and were introduced at London Airport on 1 July 1947, at Prestwick on 1 January 1948 and at Liverpool/Speke on 18 May the same year.

The Joint MCA/RAF Air Traffic Control Centre at Raigmore House, Inverness, was closed on 14 April, and the responsibilities for northern Scottish airspace was continued from Redbrae House at Prestwick.

The remains of KLM Connstellation PH-TEN scattered over Auchinweet Farm near Tarbolton after the aircraft flew into 132,000 volt National Grid power cables. [Simons Peters Collection]

On 11 June 1948, the Russians mounted a surface blockade of routes into Berlin. The Allied response was to mount a service and civilian airlift which maintained the city until the ground routes were reopened on 12 May 1949. Scottish Airlines joined Operation 'Plainfare' with two DC-3 and three Liberator aircraft. Their contribution was as follows:

		Freighter		Tanker	
		Sorties	Tons	Sorties	Tons
Dakota	G-AGWS	51	175.9		
Dakota	G-AGZF	50	172.2		
Liberator	G-AHDY			233	1534.0
Liberator	G-AHZP	15	110.1		
Liberator	G-AHZR			148	1182.5
Totals		116	458.2	381	2716.5

To handle USAF flights between the USA and Europe, the 1631st Air Base Squadron was activated at Prestwick in November 1948. Building work began on the disused aircraft dispersal sites on the north-east side of the airport, to be known as the 'Greensite' and provided full aircraft maintenance facilities and family accommodation for USAF personnel. From October 1953, the 67th Air Rescue Squadron began operations from Prestwick, initially using SB-17H aircraft. The SB-29 followed and in 1954 the HC-54D appeared, with Grumman HU-16B amphibians. In 1965, these were replaced by the HC-130H Hercules. Two Sikorsky H-19 helicopters arrived at Prestwick on 31 July 1952 after completing a transatlantic crossing. The 1631st Base Squadron opened a MATS passenger and operations building in May 1963 and from 5 August 1966 handled the regular three-times-weekly C-118 and later C-141 transports. Historic Adamton House, east of the airfield, was again occupied by the USAF, this time as the Officers' Club.

An Icelandic Airways DC-4 service from Reykjavik to London via Prestwick began in 1949 and during the year, KLM operated the first weekly all-cargo service through Prestwick to New York. BOAC introduced the Boeing Stratocruiser service on 6 December, from London to New York, via Prestwick.

The last of 3000 transatlantic crossings by BOAC Return Ferry Service Liberators between Prestwick and Montreal was completed at the end of September 1949. Since September 1946, only cargo and mail had been carried. This service continued three times per week, with Scottish Airlines providing the crews, until the B-24s were withdrawn from service in September 1949.

By 1950, weekly summer scheduled services through Prestwick totalled 79, KLM flying 27, SAS twenty, BOAC twelve, TCA seven, AOA seven, Air France three and Scottish Airlines three. On 10 June 1950, AOA replaced its Constellations with Stratocruisers on the New York-Prestwick-Amsterdam-Frankfurt route. PanAm opened an office at Prestwick and took over the AOA routes on 25 October 1950.

Following the resurfacing of the runways at Prestwick in 1949, AOA introduced the Boeing Stratocruiser via Prestwick on 31 August and the BOAC service from London to New York via Prestwick was flown by Stratocruisers from 6 December 1949. To provide additional length, 1000 feet of grass overrun to runway 13/31 was prepared in 1952 giving a total of 7600 feet. To cope with the occasional crosswind conditions on runway 13/31, a new runway, 03/21 (6000 feet by 240 feet), was constructed at the eastern end of the airfield, reaching to the disused Ayr/Heathfield site. It opened on 30 September 1955.

Scottish Air Lines flew DC-3 services on a Prestwick-Burtonwood-Northolt route in 1951 and KLM introduced a Constellation sleeper service from Amsterdam to New York, via Prestwick on 26 May. The first visit by a Comet jet airliner occurred on 5 April 1951 and a visit by the mighty Brabazon transport attracted 3000 spectators on 28 August. From 1952, Scottish Airlines operated up to eight York aircraft on trooping contracts, but these had ceased when the airline closed in 1958.

From 7 October 1953, a BOAC London to Trinidad service was opened with Constellations, via Prestwick, Gander, Bermuda and Barbados. TCA served London

The 230-foot span Bristol Brabazon, hoped by many to be the future of British airliner design, paid a visit to Prestwick on 28 August 1951 [via author]

MATS C–118A 33293 at Prestwick in 1959 [G. L. R. Macadie]

from Toronto, via Prestwick, from 1 November, with the pressurised DC-4M. TCA introduced an initial first/tourist class service on their L-1049C Constellations, from Montreal to London, via Prestwick, on 14 May 1954.

Airwork Atlantic introduced, from March 1955, a DC-4 and later a DC-6A on a twice weekly all-cargo service from London to New York via Manchester, Prestwick, Keflavik, Gander and Montreal, but the service was suspended on 18 December. During the year, BOAC leased three L-1049D to upgrade their 'Coronet' tourist service from London to New York, via Prestwick.

To cope with the increasing number of British emigrants wishing to settle in Canada, the Canadian Government chartered a number of DC-4M and Super Constellation transports from TCA, as well as DC-6Bs from Canadian Pacific. These charters were extended to DC-4s from Maritime Central and Wheeler Airlines. Following the uprising in Hungary in 1956, a large number of refugees also wished to settle in Canada. Even more capacity was now required and Flying Tiger, Slick and Great Lakes Airlines joined this 'Air Bridge' from London and Prestwick to Canada with their DC-4 transports.

By June 1957, additional DC-4 capacity was sought from General Airways, Meteor Air Transport, Californian Eastern Aviation and Overseas National Airways. Sabena also joined the 'non-skeds' with their DC-7Cs. Flights were routed from Vienna and Heathrow and via Prestwick or Shannon en-route to Edmonton, Moncton, Montreal, Toronto, Vancouver and Winnipeg. The first departures from Heathrow were on 24 November 1956 by a Maritime Central DC-4 and a Canadian Pacific DC-6B. Flights via Prestwick commenced on 15 March 1957, by DC-4s of Great Lakes, Flying Tiger and Slick. By the end of the year, some 17,656 emigrants and refugees had been flown to Canada in 207 flights. Using the last of their long-range DC-7C transports, KLM began a service from Amsterdam to New York, via Prestwick on 3 June. Signalling the end of the long-range propeller era, BOAC opened a service from London to Chicago via Prestwick, Montreal and Detroit in April 1958, using Britannia turbo-prop aircraft.

Since the requisition of the Prestwick site by the RAF in 1941 and the compulsory acquisition of Prestwick Airport by the MCA in 1946, Scottish Aviation spent many years in meetings and

Curtiss Commando of Seaboard & Western visitng Prestwick in 1959 [G. L. R. Macadie]

Seen at Prestwick on 17 June 1961 was KB–50J 6094 of the USAF's 420th Air Refuelling Squadron on a visit from Sculthorpe [G. L. R. Macadie]

litigation to recover rent allegedly due, as well as compensation for the compulsory acquisition. Not until 1953 was a settlement reached and Scottish Aviation was granted a 99-year lease on their site.

Turbo-jet services began at Prestwick on 1 June 1960, when Trans Canada introduced the DC-8-41 on the Montreal to London route. BOAC, PanAm, KLM, SAS and Seaboard & Western all brought their DC-8/B707 fleets into service through Prestwick. Both BOAC and Pan Am flew all-cargo DC-7F transports from New York to London, via Prestwick, the first on December 3. Many colourful charter flights were using Prestwick in 1962, including Capital, Riddle, Flying Tiger, Saturn, Eros, Aerlinte, Lufthansa, CPA, Sabena, Wardair and Aeroflot.

Twenty-five years of service

Prestwick celebrated its first twenty-five years of operation when in the early 1960s plans were announced for a £4 million upgrade of runway 13/31 and facilities at the airport. A new parking apron with twelve jet aircraft stands was built in front of a new passenger terminal and a well-placed new control tower was to be sited at the intersection of the two main runways. A new fire station was also planned. To accept the turbo-jet traffic of the five transatlantic operators using Prestwick, (BOAC, SAS, KLM, Pan American and TCA) runway 13/31 was lengthened to 9800 feet and opened on 17 May 1960. This extension was to cause distress, due to the closing of the Ayr-Glasgow road when take-offs and landings were taking place. A new dual carriageway was then built to the west of the terminal building to resolve these delays.

Prestwick had always been the most bad-weather-free airport in the country and this diversion status for civil and military aircraft continues to this day, but Prestwick was also the first airport in the UK to offer Duty-free purchases (from March 1959) and attracted as many as 62,000 sightseers in 1962! Although inter-Governmental Agreements provided the transatlantic carriers, the airport lacked effective connecting domestic air services until 1994.

New terminal and control tower

Construction of a new terminal building and control tower began in June 1961, and the tower was opened on 24 April 1962. The new terminal building, with a two-level 'finger', was opened by Her Majesty the Queen on 22 September 1964. A covered link to a new station on the adjacent Stranraer to Glasgow railway line was not completed until 1994, while a proposed modern transit hotel was never built. As part of the redevelopment work at the Airport, from 1960, the 'Tiger' and 'Anson' hangars were removed to increase clearance from runway 13/31. To replace this loss, SAL planned to bridge the gap between hangars 11 and 12, but with the closing and opening of aircraft maintenance contracts, this joining of the two hangars did not proceeded.

In the summer of 1964, the MCA installed arrester

Prestwick was one of the designated 'dispersal' airfields for use by the RAF V-bomber force. Here four Valiants, including XD874 of the Marham Wing, rest during a dispersal exercise[author]

Built in 1962 to replace the tower on the roof of the former Orangefield Hotel, the new control tower is seen here in December 1970 [author]

gear at the west end of runway 31 to deal with any Canadian CF-104 jet-fighters overshooting after their maintenance test flights.

PanAm operated its last DC-7C scheduled service on 27 September 1963, before it was replaced by a DC-8 via Keflavik. BOAC opened a scheduled service with B707 on 27 May 1960 with G-APFB. With high passenger demand, BOAC used the Comet 4 for its services between Prestwick and New York via Gander from August 1964. British Caledonian Airways meanwhile received approval on 1 April 1965, for inclusive tours from London to New York via Prestwick.

British Airports Authority

Together with Heathrow, Gatwick and Stansted, British Airports Authority (BAA), took over the facilities at Prestwick Airport on 1 April, including the air cargo and handling services. Air cargo services with Pan American B707s began in 1964 and BOAC introduced their services in 1966. Air cargo through Prestwick had increased tenfold from 1000 tonnes in 1951 to 10,000 tonnes by 1966.

In June 1966, the USAF Air Rescue Squadron, by now equipped with HC-130 aircraft, was relocated to Moron AFB in Spain, vacating the 'Greensite' area at Prestwick. The MATS terminal continued at Prestwick until the last C-141 departed on 31 March 1992.

From 13 January 1966, BOAC operated all-cargo services with B707-320C transports, from London to New York via Manchester and Prestwick. BOAC introduced the Super VC-10 G–ASGD onto its London to Montreal and Chicago service, via Prestwick on 1 April 1966.

SAS and KLM terminated their Prestwick scheduled passenger stops in October 1968 and October 1969 respectively.

Prestwick's record of fog-free diversion status was put to the test in December 1969, when on the 9th, sixteen international flights were diverted to the Airport, due weather. Three days later a total of 59 diversions were handled.

Prestwick Airport's future

From time to time, the future role of Prestwick Airport was raised in discussions between local business interest and the BAA. The recent Bermuda 2 Agreement between Britain and the United States included the recognition of Prestwick as the designated 'gateway' to Scotland for scheduled and charter air services, but this status was not matched by the benefit of frequent domestic or continental connecting services.

DC–7C N90804 of US supplimental carrier Saturn Airways at Prestwick in September 1966. It flew transatlantic charters until being withdrawn in 1968 [author]

Dakota F–BAXR of Rousseau Aviation at Prestwick on 16 August 1968. This operator flew 'XR until 1972, and it was scrapped four years later [author]

Orangefield terminal demolished

To provide a clear access for the construction of the remaining section of the parallel taxi-track to the south of runway 13/31, the historic Orangefield Hotel and surrounding area was demolished in 1966. The 'Greensite' area and maintenance and accommodation facilities recently vacated by the USAF Rescue Squadron were taken over by the Royal Navy and commissioned as HMS Gannet on 23 November 1970 and 819 Squadron of Sea Kings arrived to provide anti-submarine defence and support for the British and US Navy Polaris submarine fleets in the Clyde estuary. They also added a search and rescue role for both military and civil incidents. From 1972, RAF personnel from the Scottish Military Area Control Centre were housed within the complex.

By 1970, BOAC, Air Canada, SAS and Seaboard operated air-cargo services through Prestwick and the annual total accounted for 15,000 tonnes, with a value of £97 million. Prestwick was visited by the first Boeing 747 'Jumbo' jets in August 1970, with BOAC's G-AWNC on the 1st and PanAm flight PA120 diverted in with 333 passengers, due to fog at Heathrow, on the 3rd.

In the summer of 1971, runway 13/31 at Prestwick was resurfaced and strengthened to accept all types of 'Jumbo' military and civil passenger and cargo transports. By this time, the area of the airport had grown to 1299 acres (526 hectares) and, including British Aerospace, some 1500 persons were employed. On 28 June, Concorde 002 gave a fly-by to 13,000 people at the airport. The first USAF MATS C-5A Galaxy aircraft landed at Prestwick on 2 February 1972, on diversion from Mildenhall.

For the Summer of 1972, BOAC introduced a Boeing 747 service from Manchester and Prestwick to New York. The last scheduled flight by SAS was with DC-8 LN-MOC on 31 October 1972.

On 7 April 1973, Laker Airways began operating DC-10 charter services from Prestwick, and from 1 June, British Caledonian opened a daily London-Manchester Prestwick service to New York. However, the fuel crisis in 1974 resulted in the cut-back of many charter services. The fuel crisis also affected PanAm services through Prestwick, which were terminated on 2 January 1974, but cargo services continued with Boeing 747 freighters. BOAC opened a 747 scheduled service to Toronto on 27 May, 1974. On 12 May 1976, 68 charter flights brought 11,000 football fans to the European Cup final.

A large plaque of the airport was unveiled by the Duke of Hamilton in the international departure lounge at Prestwick on 25 January 1973, commemorating the Orangefield Hotel and terminal building and the many services it provided during its long

A frequent visitor to Prestwick was Grumman Turbo-Goose G–ASXG, seen here in May 1970 when carrying passengers to a fishing holiday in the Scottish lochs [author]

Seen at Prestwick in June 1970 was DC–4 N529D of Carolina Aircraft Corporation, who operated this aircraft from December 1969 to October 1970. Its large cargo doors indicate its original service as a C–54 of the USAAF [author]

C–124 Globemaster I 0-21044 of the Tennessee Air National Guard at Prestwick on 25 August 1970 when on its way to Frankfurt. This was one of many USAF aircraft using Prestwick as a staging post [author]

life. The aviation murals which once graced the hotel walls are now preserved in a nearby indoor bowling green, and the maple floor from the hotel dining room was relaid in the conference room in the terminal.

In 1975, an updated ILS system was installed at both ends of runway 13/31 and new approach and runway lighting was installed.

Airliner crew training is a continuing feature at Prestwick, but a serious accident occurred on 17 March, 1977, when BOAC Boeing 707 G-APFK crashed on take-off from runway 13. After coming to rest near the tower and fire station, the airliner was written-off.

Air Canada introduced L-1011 Tristars and Boeing 747s on its Prestwick schedules from 24 April 1977 and Wardair began a weekly Boeing 747 ABC charter service. In the following year, British Caledonian began an air-cargo service through Prestwick. Northwest Airlines inaugurated a daily Copenhagen to Seattle service, via Prestwick, Boston and Minneapolis from 9 June 1978, using Boeing 747 and later DC-10 transports. Northwest added a Boston to Copenhagen 747 cargo service to its Prestwick operation on 11 February 1979, while Pan American withdrew its air-cargo services from Prestwick that year.

Air cargo services at Prestwick received a boost when Flying Tigers introduced a weekly scheduled DC-8F service between Prestwick and New York in August 1981. This was joined by a Boeing 747F service in 1982. In January 1982, airlines operating through Prestwick included Laker and Wardair (DC-10), Northwest (B.747/B.747F), Flying Tiger (DC-8F/B.747F), Airtours (Tristar), Air Canada (Tristar/DC-8/DC-8F), World, Canadian Pacific, Trans America (DC-8), Arrow Air (B.707), British Airways (B.747) and British Caledonian (DC-10/B.707F). However, Laker collapsed in February 1982, which was a sad loss to Prestwick. In August 1983,

Tu.104 CCCP-42448 of Aeroflot at Prestwick on 30 August 1970 when on a service to Moscow [via author]

Pan Am's Boeing 707–321C N446PA 'Clipper Climax' at Prestwick on 16 May 1970. Flight time to New York was 7 to 8 hours depending on weather. Parked behind Pan-Am is a BOAC VC-10 and 707. [author]

British Airways severed its wartime links with Prestwick when its services were terminated, and Scottish transatlantic passengers were added to the Glasgow-Heathrow 'shuttle'.

Passenger charter flights continued through Prestwick during the 1980s and in 1986 were noted as services to Boston, Chicago and New York were being flown by American Transair (L-1101), Prestwick to Toronto by British Airtours (L-1011), Prestwick to Toronto and Winnipeg by Nationair (DC-8-63), Prestwick to Toronto by Quebec Air (DC-8-63), Prestwick to Toronto, Calgary and Vancouver by Wardair (B.747) and Prestwick to Toronto and Vancouver by Worldways (DC-8-63 and Tristar). A new airline, Highland Express attempted a Boeing 747 service from Prestwick to New York in 1988, but went into liquidation after only five months of operations.

To save rating expenditure, runway 03/21 was closed in 1985, but with the commencement of flying training by the new British Aerospace Flying Training College, a short length was later reopened. The British Aerospace Flying College began operations at Prestwick on 20 May 1988, its fleet of training aircraft including twelve Bravos, thirty Cherokees and ten Senecas. The College was formally opened on 24 November and the fleet of training aircraft is housed in the refurbished prewar 'Fokker' hangar.

Run-down again

Following a review of the operations at the Scottish Lowland airports (Prestwick, Abbotsinch and Turnhouse) on 6 May 1990, exclusive transatlantic gateway status was removed from Prestwick Airport. This had the immediate result of Northwest Airlines moving their Prestwick-Boston service to Abbotsinch, followed by the Air Canada service to Toronto on 16 May. Air Canada cargo remained at Prestwick for the time being. With the closing of the

Abover: The Minnesota Air National Guard flew C–97G 0–30270 into Prestwick in 1970 [G. L. R. Macadie]

Ilyushin Il–62 CCCP–86676, which visited Prestwick on 18 May 1970, was typical of the growing number of 'iron curtain' aircraft seen at the airport [author]

Prestwick Airport terminal building, March 1971 [author]

US Navy Polaris base at nearby Holy Loch, the last of the regular USAF MATS charter services departed in October 1991. Reduction in business at the airport also resulted in the closing of the airport shop and post office, the bank having shut down some years previously.

During the first three months of 1990 only 6900 passengers and 4729 tonnes of cargo had been handled.

Prestwick Airport purchased

To safeguard flying operations, on 1 April 1992, Prestwick Airport was purchased from BAA by British Aerospace. A number of local business interests (ACAP) acquired the terminal building and facilities south of the main runway and the runway itself was leased from British Aerospace. Passenger and cargo facilities were now to be operated by PIK International Ltd., which began operations with just 51 employees. A hard period of returning the airport to a working, profitable operation was begun, every aspect of the airport operation being examined, and plans were laid for rebuilding of the airport facilities and services. The retention of Air Cargo was an important first step and in June, Federal Express (Fedex) acquired a 10% stake in PIK and signed a ten-year lease for their cargo facility. Runway 03/21 had its 6000 feet reinstated for crosswind landings. Plans are in hand for an extension to allow all-weather landings by cargo-carrying Boeing 747s.

On 1 February 1993, PIK took over the handling of all aircraft from Ogden Aviation and from 1 April replaced the staff at the CAA-operated control tower with their own air traffic controllers and support staff. To attract more passengers to the airport, PIK applied for planning approval to construct a railway halt on the Stranraer-Ayr-Glasgow railway line, with a covered air-bridge to the airport. This was a very similar facility to that shown on the terminal building drawings in 1960 and 1963, and work began on 29 November 1993.

The spectators' terrace was reopened in June and the rail halt, with its covered air-bridge to the terminal building, was opened on 5 September 1994. Free train connections between any manned station in Scotland and Prestwick Airport was offered to departing passengers. Arriving passengers are charged just £5.00

Piper PA–28–180G Cherokee G–AZSG, seen in August 1973, was the first aircraft delivered to Prestwick Flying Group. Apart for flying tuition, it was used for general touring purposes. Note the spectators leaning over the balcony railing! [author]

Catalina amphibian N4760C of Geoterrex was used as an aerial survey aircraft, and featured a magnetic anomaly detector stalk in the rear fuselage. It made use of Prestwick's facilities in August 1976 [author]

Based at HMS Gannet, Prestwick, for many years have been the Sea Kings of 819 Squadron of the Fleet Air Arm. Here XV674 is seen in July 1978 during a Flying Club open day [author]

for a journey to any station in Scotland. An additional 1000 space car park was opened adjacent to the train halt on 15 April 1995. A new western fire station was opened in 1996, but from August, in a bid to hold operating costs, the airport was closed from 2300 to 0700 daily. To add a further commercial 'signature' to the west of Scotland airports, the designation Glasgow/Paisley and Glasgow/Prestwick International Airports was announced.

Air Canada cargo flights gained traffic rights from Prestwick to Zurich and Dusseldorf and air cargo at the airport totalled 16,000 tonnes in 1992. A new western fire station was opened in December 1992, as was an apron services building. With the withdrawal of Canadian Armed Forces from Europe, it was announced that CAF transit flights would continue to use Prestwick as their forward strategic staging post in Europe.

At the end of 1993, regular air-cargo services from Prestwick were being flown by Federal Express Boeing 747s, Air Canada DC-8Fs and Polar Air Cargo Boeing 747Fs, with additional cargo and passengers charters. The Air Canada DC-8F cargo service through Prestwick was terminated on 26 March, 1994, cargo being roaded to Glasgow to join passenger services to Toronto. A new cargo service by Cargolux Boeing 747F began two days later, from Luxembourg to Seattle. Lufthansa also opened a Frankfurt to Chicago service on 25 April with B747F.

Long-awaited continental and domestic passenger services from Prestwick began on 3 May 1994, when Ryanair opened a twice-daily service to Dublin with Boeing 737 aircraft. This service increased to three services daily from the following May.

Prestwick maintained its reputation as a weather diversion airport when eighteen flights were diverted on 27 January 1995, thirteen from Glasgow Airport, four from Edinburgh and one from Aberdeen. In the mid-1990s there was some argument about the airport's name, but it was finally agreed that it would be Glasgow/Prestwick.

In addition to scheduled air-cargo services by Cargolux, Lufthansa and Federal Express, passenger

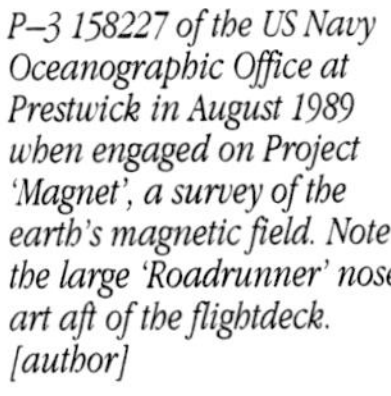

P–3 158227 of the US Navy Oceanographic Office at Prestwick in August 1989 when engaged on Project 'Magnet', a survey of the earth's magnetic field. Note the large 'Roadrunner' nose art aft of the flightdeck. [author]

charter traffic during the summer of 1995 was provided by American Trans Air (Tristar), Air Transat (Tristar/B.757) and Caledonian (A320). A three times per day service between Belfast and Prestwick were commenced by Gill Airways on 3 July 1995 and from 27 October Ryanair began a four flights per service between Prestwick and London (Stansted). These services attracted a healthy response from the travelling public. By October 1995, 68 services per week were scheduled between Prestwick, Dublin, London and Belfast and by the end of the year, passengers using the airport increased to 340,000, including 65,000 passengers to or from Dublin, 50,000 to or from Belfast and 225,000 between Prestwick and Stansted. These improvements continued in 1996, with Laker Airways returning to the Prestwick to Orlando route in May. It was noted that from 20 May 62 arrivals and departures were scheduled each day, from Laker (DC-10), Cargolux (B.747), Ryanair (B.737), Air Transat (Tristar), Gill (SD360), Fedex (MD11), FUA, TWE and Lufthansa (B.747). In December 1996, the following services were logged during the month; Air France six B.747F, Cargolux seventeen B.747F, Lufthansa eleven B.747F, Federal Express 27 DC-10/MD11/B.727, Gill 74 SD360/ATR42/ATR72, and Ryanair 175 B.737. At the end of 1996, Prestwick had handled 542,000 passengers and 40,000 tonnes of cargo.

New cargo terminal

On Monday 15 December 1997, ground was broken at Prestwick on the site of an £8m project for a new cargo terminal. Located south of the parallel taxi-track, the facility offers nose-in parking for a range of transport aircraft. 50 wide-bodied cargo flights were being handled each week and a four-fold increase in cargo traffic was expected by the year 2002. A new cargo village providing 145,000 sq. ft. (13475 sq. m.) of capacity was opened on 22 December 1998. Instant nationwide trans-shipment direct from cargo aircraft to vehicle was commenced, with Debsmith European Transport, Concorde Express, Plane Trucking, Sutherlands and Ron Smith transport. Glasgow (Prestwick) Airport ended the financial year in March 1998, with a turnover of £21.7 million, making a £2.2 million profit and employing 385 people.

Services for summer 1998 included scheduled services to Belfast by Gill Airways, Dublin and London (Stansted) by Ryanair, charter services to Jersey by Brymon, Bulgaria by Air Via, Ibiza and Majorca by Air Europe, Majorca by Air Futura, Turkey by Pegasus, Toronto by Air Transat, and Detroit and Florida by American Transair.

New training contracts saw the addition of the USAF C-20 (Learjet 35A) and C-21A (Gulfstream 3 & 4) military aircraft as well as airline types from British Midland. Ryanair confirmed their summer 1998 schedules with four daily flights to Dublin and five to Stansted. 19 November 1998 saw the much sought after inauguration of a twice-daily direct Ryanair service from Prestwick to Beauvais (for Paris). Adding yet again to its services, Ryanair began a new daily Prestwick to Frankfurt air service on 26 March 2000.

On the last day of April 1998, the Stagecoach transport conglomerate acquired a 75% holding in Glasgow (Prestwick) Airport for £41m. The remaining 25% of this joint venture is held by Executive Chairman, Matthew Hudson. The new division, Stagecoach Aviation, now operates the airport and related businesses. Early in 1999, Stagecoach completed the new air cargo terminal and passenger arrivals hall, resurfaced runway 03/21 with new lighting and began construction of a large Boeing 747-size maintenance hangar for Polar Air Cargo. With increasing numbers of schedules and en-route aircraft movements, PIK returned the airport to 24-hour operation in early 1998, there being three short rest periods during the night.

Using the new cargo terminal on 16 August 1999 was Cargolux Boeing 747F LX–GCV of Cargolux [author]

Above: Glasgow/Prestwick Airport from the air in 1999. Not as busy as in 1945 but interesting nevertheless [author]
Below: Prestwick's new cargo terminal photographed in June 2000 [HMS Gannet]

Typical of the 'bizjets' using Prestwick is Learjet 60 N139XX. This aircraft is based there for air charter work, and was photographed on 22 July 1999 [author]

The rise, decline and rise of Prestwick's business can be illustrated by the following figures:

1951: 128,000 passengers + 1000 tons of cargo
1961 198,795 passengers + 2935 tons of cargo
1970: 335,131 passengers + 15,886 tons of cargo
1980: 393,600 passengers
1985: 237,700 passengers + 11,671 tons of cargo
1992: 11,000 passengers + 16,000 tons of cargo
1995: 340,000 passengers + 39,500 tons of cargo
1999: 675,000 passengers + 53,500 tons of cargo
2000: 800,000 passengers + 55,000 tons of cargo (est)

Scottish Aviation manufacturing 1943 - 1998

Following the early aircraft maintenance and manufacturing work at Prestwick already described, 1943 saw Scottish Aviation busily working on Spitfires and sub-contract work, as well as modifications to B-17, B-24, B-25 and C-47 aircraft. Factory floor space had increased from 29,500 square feet in 1938 to 845,000 feet by 1945.

During the 1940s, fluctuating availability of work for SAL caused concern. In January 1944, Douglas McIntyre again visited Consolidated in the United States and gained approval for modifications to the Liberator should SAL decide to build a new civil transport fuselaged version. They then supplied a small number of conversions of the wartime Liberator bomber to 24-seat civil transports. McIntyre also signed a Letter of Agreement with TWA, should Scottish Airlines begin transatlantic air services.

SAL also gained a licence agreement with the Douglas Aircraft Company to consolidate its war-time role as design authority for the repair, overhaul and conversion of C-47/DC-3 Dakota and C-54/DC-4 Skymaster aircraft to civil transports. A first order for five conversions to DC-3 standard came from Royal Dutch Airlines (KLM) and was followed by many more. In 1950, SAL converted 38 BEA Dakotas to the 32-seat 'Pionair' Class transport for domestic and continental routes. In total, nearly 300 DC-3 and DC-4 transports were converted for civil use. In December 1945, SAL also acquired the rights for the overhaul of Pratt & Whitney aero engines and of instruments made by the Sperry

Steady streams of C–5A Galaxy heavy transport aircraft staged through Prestwick during the 1999 Kosovo conflict. This picture of 00460, however, was taken ten years earlier [author]

Polar Air Cargo's new maintenance hangar nearing completion in June 2000. Three RAF Hercules aircraft are prominent in the foreground [HMS Gannet]

Gyroscope Company. From 1961, Rolls-Royce Merlin and Griffon aero engines were added to the engine overhaul business. Scottish Air Engine Services were housed in the prewar 'Tiger' hangar. By 1966, SAL had taken over all maintenance work of Rolls-Royce piston engines and when this work finally came to an end in 1981, SAES had overhauled 1,910 Griffon engines.

In November 1954, SAL began a series of aircraft maintenance contracts for the Royal Canadian Air Force (later renamed Canadian Armed Forces) at their site at Renfrew airport. At first, the aircraft overhauled were CF-100, F-86 Sabre jet-fighters and T-33A Shooting Star trainers. In the summer of 1960, this work was transferred to Prestwick and work on the CF-5A soon followed, with from January 1963, CF-104 jet fighters. The 1000th completion was in December 1967, and these contacts were completed in 1978.

Prestwick Pioneer and Twin Pioneer

In February 1945, Scottish Aviation submitted a design study to meet Air Ministry Specification A.4/45 for a light, three-seat cabin, high-wing monoplane for communication with officers in the field. The aircraft was to be of robust construction and suitable for landing on rough surfaces and small landing grounds. Design work began and on 5 November 1947 VL515, the prototype Pioneer, powered by a 240hp DH Gipsy Queen engine, was flown. Converted to a four-seat, Series 2, now powered by a 520hp Alvis Leonides engine, it was flown on 5 May 1950 as G-AKBF /G-31-1). 59 Pioneers were sold to the RAF as well as to the Ceylonese and Malaysian Air Forces. VL516 was the first Pioneer delivered to the RAF, in September 1953, and RAF Pioneers were to see much service in the jungles of Malaya during unrest in 1954/55 and were not withdrawn until 1968.

A larger, twin-engined design, the 16-seat Twin Pioneer followed and the prototype was first flown on 25 June 1955 as G-ANTP. A Certificate of Airworthiness was issued in November 1956 but during a demonstration tour in North Africa with Twin Pioneer G-AOEO, David McIntyre and his crew were lost on 7 December 1957, following structural failure of the main strut fitting. After modification, production continued and the the first aircraft of an order for 39 for the RAF, XL966, was flown on 29 August 1957. A variety of civil operators purchased the remainder of the 87 Twin Pioneers to be built, the last in 1962.

A new large 'Britannia' hangar of 45,000 sq. ft.(4182 sq. m.) was built in 1965, to provide adequate space for future maintenance and conversion work for a wide

The Scottish Aviation factory at Prestwick in 1946. The proximity of the end of runway 14 is interesting! [D. McIntyre]

range of aircraft types. In the 1960s, several Convair 240s were upgraded with the fitting of Rolls-Royce Dart turboprops to Convair 600 standard, Britannias were refurbished for Laker Airways and cargo doors were fitted to Aer Lingus Viscounts. SAL Check was formed in June 1962 as an approved aircraft overhaul, repair and maintenance service and was to continue in operation for many years. Also in 1962, twelve former Fleet Air Arm Skyraider aircraft were converted as target-tugs for the Swedish Air Force. In 1968 the Department handled a total of 566 aircraft maintenance contracts.

In 1965, Scottish Aviation gained contracts to build the wings for Handley-Page Jetstreams and in 1966, 20-foot long sections of Lockheed C-130 fuselages as well as the under-wing fuel tank pylons. The Hercules work was sited in the prewar 'Fokker' hangar and on completion of the contract in 1982, 773 sets of C-130 fuselage panels had been dispatch to Lockheed.

Bulldog trainer

Beagle Aircraft had developed a successor to the early Beagle Pup light trainer and had secured an order for 58 Bulldogs from the Royal Swedish Air Force. G–AXEH, the first Bulldog, converted from a Pup, had made its first flight on 19 May 1969, but flight tests were not completed as Beagle went into receivership in early 1970. Scottish Aviation were quick to enter into negotiations with the

Above: SAL Pioneer XL517 was typical of the type, and is seen in service with the RAF in the Far East in September 1964 [via P. Spencer]

Left: Scottish Aviation's second design was the Twin Pioneer, an example of which, XL970, is seen serving in Malaysia in 1968 [via P. Spencer]

SAL Bulldogs were built at Prestwick for the RAF and other air arms, and here XX700 is seen at Waddington in October 1994 [J. F. Hamlin]

Receiver and acquired the design, production and marketing rights for the Bulldog, as well as support for the other Beagle designs, the Pup, Basset and Beagle 206.

The production team at Prestwick went to work on the new design and the second prototype was moved to Prestwick for completion. It was first flown on 14 February 1971 as G-AXIG. The first production Bulldog was flown on 21 June 1971 (G-AYWN/Swedish 61001) and was delivered on 26 July. SAL went on to build ninety Bulldogs for the Sweden Army and Air Force, and this was followed by orders for 132 more for the RAF, to replace the Chipmunk basic trainer, as well as orders from Malaysia, Kenya, Ghana, Nigeria, Jordan, Lebanon, Hong Kong and Botswana, for a total of 324 Bulldogs.

SAL taken over by Cammell Laird

In April 1966, it was announced that Scottish Aviation had been taken over by shipbuilders Cammell Laird, which, in a declining ship-building market, was diversifying into other fields. A 75% stake in a new company to market the Bell 47 helicopter was not a success, due to the number of cheap ex-military aircraft available.

Handley Page Jetstream

The Cammell Laird take-over of Scottish Aviation allowed investment in a far-reaching project. Handley Page was developing a small, twin-engined 18-seat airliner and required a sub- contractor to manufacture the wing sets. SAL was successful in this tender and received a contract to produce 54 sets of wings, the first two being delivered in October 1967. G–ATXH, the first Astazou-powered Jetstream, flew at Radlett on 18 August, 1967. This construction programme became too much for the financial base of Handley Page and the Company was forced into receivership on 7 August 1969, by which time some 25 Jetstreams were in service. Jetstream wing production ceased at Prestwick on 27 February 1970 and in April Handley Page went into liquidation.

An American entrepreneur, Bill Bright, acquired the rights as Jetstream Aircraft Limited, including the prototype of a Garrett-engine C-10A transport for the USAF. This prototype, G-AWBL, had flown on 21 November 1968.

With the resulting payment difficulties from Handley Page and indeed the collapse of Rolls-Royce at this time, Scottish Aviation was left in a perilous position. The saving grace for Scottish Aviation at Prestwick came from another failure in the British aircraft industry.

Military Jetstreams - and nationalisation

In 1970, the RAF had stated a requirement for a multi-engined training aircraft. Scottish Aviation looked at the potential for the Jetstream for this contract and acquired the rights from Bill Bright. A tender was placed by SAL for the contract and, on 24 February 1972 the Government awarded them the contract for 26 aircraft. SAL found they had fifteen sets of completed wings, with seven more in assembly. The tail unit of the Jetstream was already under sub-contract to North West Industries of Canada. Three Handley Page-built fuselages were completed and a further eleven were in storage. In addition, seven fuselages were partly completed, which left Scottish Aviation needing five new fuselages to complete the contract. After looking for a sub-contractor for this work, SAL decided to set up a production line for these fuselages.

On Friday 13 April 1973, the first Astazou-powered Jetstream for the RAF, XX475, was flown and was delivered on 26 June. To delay the delivery of the contract, it was agreed that the last ten aircraft would be

Production of the Jetstream was taken over by SAL from Handley Page when that company failed. XX498 (left) was one of those used by the RAF [J. F. Hamlin]

The highly-developed Jetstream 41 in the shape of G–PJRT (below), at Farnborough in 1992 [author]

for civil use, followed by ten new aircraft for the RAF. In October 1976, SAL began a contract to convert sixteen of the RAF Jetstreams for 750 Squadron at RNAS Culdrose, the Fleet Air Arm Observer School.

The Labour victory in the General Election of 1974 led to the amalgamation and nationalisation of most of the units of the British aircraft industry. At first Scottish Aviation was excluded, due to its lower financial turnover, but following representations to the Government, on 1 January 1978 SAL became a division of British Aerospace.

British Caledonian announced in January 1978 its intention to site a £8 million engine overhaul facility on the Shawfarm Estate to the south of the airport. From 1980, an increasing number of General Electric CF-6 engines were overhauled for operators of Boeing 747, Airbus and DC-10 transports. This facility continues in the 1990s as General Electric Caledonian, with the addition of the CFM-56 turbo-fan.

BAe Jetstream

Before nationalisation, the SAL Board had considered the development of the Garrett-powered Jetstream. The power-plant of the 57 Astazou Jetstreams in service had received criticism, particularly in the United States, where some airframes had already been given Garrett power-plants. Since the first design of the Jetstream, deregulation had allowed regional airline operators to fly passengers into large 'hub' airports, for which they required a pressurised, modern, Jetstream-sized transport.

British Aerospace gave approval for the development of the Jetstream 31 in January 1981 and an early Handley-Page 200 series airframe was purchased from the Unites States (N510F) to be used as a development aircraft. Garrett-powered prototype G-JSSD, was first flown on 28 March 1980. The first production aircraft, G–TALL, was flown on 18 March and was awarded a Certificate of Airworthiness on 29 July. An American Approved Type Certificate followed on 1 December. More than 100 Jetstreams had been sold by August 1985, 85 to North America. Some 386 Jetstreams 31/32 had been flown when production ceased in 1997.

In November 1985, design work began on a longer 29-seat Jetstream 41 version. When first flown on 25 September 1991 as G-GCJL, this model had attracted 26 orders. The Certificate of Airworthiness was granted on 23 November.

British Aerospace announced in June 1997 that Jetstream production would end at the end of the year, due to the state of world markets and competition from some foreign manufacturers enjoying state subsidies. In all, 103 Jetstream 41s were completed, the last leaving Prestwick on 26 March 1998. Later in the year, two Jetstream 41s were delivered to the Hong Kong Government with the addition of a ventral radar dome and internal equipment for the Maritime Reconnaissance and Air Sea Rescue role.

British Aerospace celebrated 21 years of operation at Prestwick in April 1998. General Manager Tom Williams reported that the 1000 employees were now concentrating on supporting the Twin Pioneer, Bulldog and Jetstream operators as well as manufacturing parts for the military Nimrod, the Toulouse-assembled Airbus and Boeing 747 engine pylon contracts.

When this photograph was taken in September 1965 the Scottish & Oceanic Control Centre was operating from Redbrae House, pictured here festooned with aerials and with a number of ugly extensions [author]

Air Traffic Control at Prestwick 1959 - 1998

Following the wartime years and early postwar period already described, a new Scottish Airways and Prestwick Oceanic Operations Room was opened in a wartime Seco hut adjacent to Redbrae House in 1959. The Scottish Airways position was on a raised dais and carried Sector One (DCS/TLA), Sector Two (MAC/SKP) and Sector Five (FIR) positions.

An early application of computers to oceanic control was begun at the Prestwick Centre in December 1961, when an Apollo computer was installed later, with on-line flight data exchange between the Prestwick and Gander Oceanic Control Centres. Permanent controller-to-

Controllers hard at work in the Scottish & Oceanic Air Traffic Control Centre in Atlantic House, Prestwick, in 1979 [author]

controller telephone links between Gander and Prestwick were established.

The first civil ATC radar to operate in Scotland came into service in 1963, when the MCA took over the RAF long-range radar station at Gailes on the Ayrshire coast. This worked in conjunction with the procedural 'D' controllers at Redbrae House. Airfield control radars were also installed at Renfrew, Prestwick and, later, Edinburgh airports.

Increases in transatlantic crossings to 68,191 in 1964 and the replacement of the last of the propeller transports by turbo-jets showed the need for a specialist approach to both communication and air traffic services. The ICAO Council therefore agreed to establish a permanent North Atlantic Systems Planning Group (NAT SPG) on 15 April 1965, based in the Paris office.

At their first meeting in October 1965, two major changes in the direction of the control and communication responsibilities took place. The first of these was that the North Atlantic ground-air-ground communication service was to be provided by Shannon. A complementary air traffic control service was to be provided by Prestwick, resulting in today's Shanwick Control and Shanwick Radio call-signs. The British Nartel radio station at Birdlip was closed on 13 January 1966, leaving Shanwick Aeradio at Ballygirreen in Ireland as the sole European communication station serving the eastern North Atlantic routes.

The Oceanic Control Centre at Shannon was closed and Prestwick assumed the responsibility for the control of westbound North Atlantic traffic, issuing clearances to transatlantic flights planning to cross the Shanwick OCA from the eastern boundary longitudes within latitudes 61°N to 45°N.

A long-range Secondary Surveillance Radar (SSR), with a link into the Redbrae Airways Operation Room, was installed at Stornoway in 1970, providing positive cover to transponder-equipped air traffic over a large part of the North West approaches.

Transatlantic ATC remained at Redbrae House in Scotland for 31 years, until 5 April 1972, when the Oceanic Control Centre was moved to Atlantic House in the town of Prestwick. The improved working environment was soon matched by improved inter-centre communications and the first use of computers to prepare flight progress strips.

With the completion of a new Scottish Airways Centre at Atlantic House, the wartime radar station at Gailes was closed, as were the Procedural Sectors at 'Redbrae' House. From 2 November 1978 the radar and procedural controllers worked side-by-side in their new environment. Redbrae House and its 1943 Seco huts were all demolished in just two days. The radar station at Gailes was demolished, with one of the radar heads being later displayed at the Museum of Flight, East Fortune.

Computer operations in real time were introduced at Prestwick on 31 March 1987, which led to a radical change in the air traffic control operations, the ubiquitous flight progress strips, in world-wide use for some 50 years, giving way to a visual display unit, keyboard and printer input and output devices. This fundamental change in ATC operating techniques had a similar impact to the change in aircraft instrument design from the Douglas DC-3 to the 'glass cockpit' displays of the Boeing 767, Airbus and MD-10 transports.

In May 1989, Shanwick began issuing oceanic clearances in response to voice requests to suitably-equipped westbound aircraft by ACARS-SITA AIRCOM ground-based VHF link. Air Canada, TWA, American, KLM, Hapag-Lloyd, BA, Delta, United, Air France, US Air, Lufthansa and Finnair soon joined the trials.

Between the early TAC days of 1941 and the end of 1999, the Oceanic Control Centre at Prestwick has controlled some 6,500,000 flights. Total transatlantic flights in 1999 were 334,301, with a record 1108 crossings on 11 July, when aircraft were crossing the boundaries at the rate of 118 per hour. July was the busiest month, with 32,416 flights.

OFFICIAL NAME - Prestwick LOCAL NAME - Prestwick

COUNTY: South Ayrshire
LOCATION: 3 mls NNE of Ayr
LANDMARKS: Coast to W; Lady Island 5.5 mls WNW; Ayr 3.5 mls SSW; town 4.5 mls NW
GRID REF: NS365268
LAT: 55° 30' 30" N
LONG: 04° 35' 30"W
CONTROL TOWER: Wartime tower on roof of Orangefield Hotel terminal bldg; new tower in 4.62
HEIGHT ASL: 35 ft
LIGHTING: 13/31: approach, threshold and runway
03/21: threashold & runway

AIRFIELD CODE: PI (1945); later PW
EN ROUTE CODE: GGBA (1946); EGPK (1964-date)
OBSTACLES: Terminal buildings; hangars; church SW
RUNWAYS originally: 3750 ft. grass
1945: 14/32 6600 ft. x 300 ft. concrete
08/26 4500 ft x 300 ft. concrete
currently: 13/31 9800 ft. x 150 ft. conc/asphalt
03/21 6000 ft. x 150 ft. asphalt
HARDSTANDINGS: -
HOUSING: RAF and RN personnel
HANGARS: Four Bellman, two B.1 (wartime)
OPENED : 1933
CLOSED: current

MILITARY FLYING UNITS PRESENT AT PRESTWICK

UNIT	CODE	FROM	DATE IN	DATE OUT	TO	AIRCRAFT USED
12 E&RFTS		(formed)	17.2.36	3.9.39	(to 12 EFTS)	DH82; Hart; Demon; Hind;Battle; Anson; Fokker F.XXII, XXXVI
1 CANS		(formed)	15.8.38	1.11.39	(to 1 AO&NS)	Anson
12 EFTS		(ex 12 E&RFTS)	3.9.39	22.3.41	(disbanded)	Tiger Moth
1 AO&NS		(ex 1 CANS)	1.11.39	19.7.41	(disbanded)	Anson; DH89; Fokker F.XXXVI
10 AO&NS		Grangemouth	27.11.39	2.12.39	(to 1 AO&NS)	Anson
603 Sqn	XT	Turnhouse	16.12.39	14.4.40	Drem	Spitfire
610 Sqn	DW	Wittering	4.4.40	10.5.40	Biggin Hill	Spitfire
825 Sqn	G5	HMS Glorious	21.4.40	1.5.40	Worthy Down	Swordfish
141 Sqn	TW	West Malling	21.7.40	30.8.40	Turnhouse	Defiant
253 Sqn	SW	Turnhouse	23.8.40	16.9.40	Kenley	Hurricane
615 Sqn	KW	Kenley	29.8.40	10.10.40	Northolt	Hurricane
102 Sqn	DY	Leeming	1.9.40	10.10.40	Linton-on-Ouse	Whitley
4 FPP / FP (ATA)		(formed)	9.40	31.10.45	(disbanded)	Anson; Argus
1 Sqn RCAF	YO	Northolt	10.10.40	8.12.40	Castletown	Hurricane
AI/ASV School		(formed)	24.10.40	27.12.40	(became 3 RS)	Blenheim
800 Sqn		Crail	27.10.40	31.10.40	HMS Ark Royal	Skua
602 Sqn	ZT	Westhampnett	17.12.40	15.4.41	Ayr	Spitfire
3 Radio School		(ex AI/ASV Sch.)	27.12.40	19.8.42	(to 3 RDFS)	Blenheim; Botha; Hart; Anson; Audax
Glasgow UAS		(formed)	4.41	2.43	Renfrew	Tiger Moth
807 Sqn		Yeovilton	4.2.41	7.2.41	Abbotsinch	Fulmar
6 AACU det.		Ringway	3.41	6.41	Ringway	various
1527 BAT Flt.		(formed)	29.10.41	15.9.45	(to 1527 RAT Flt.)	Hudson; Oxford
1425 Flt.		(formed)	30.10.41	5.4.42	Lyneham	Liberator; Wellington; Ventura
3 RDF School		(ex 3 RS)	19.8.42	1.12.42	Hooton Park	Botha; Blenheim; Hart; DH82
1680 Flt.	MJ	Abbotsinch	6.3.44	7.2.46	(disbanded)	DH89; Wellington;Walrus; Anson; Dakota; Harrow; Fokker F.XXII
1527 (RAT) Flt.	PY	(ex 1527 BAT Flt)	15.9.45	28.2.46	(disbanded)	Oxford
Station Flight	SC	(formed)	?	?	(disbanded)	?
1631st Air Base		(formed)	11.48	6.66	(disbanded)	C-47; C-54; T-33
67th ARS		?	10.53	2.66	Moron, Spain	SC-54; SB-17H SB-29; HC-54D; HU-16B; C-130
820 Sqn		Culdrose	10.5.71	21.5.71	Culdrose	Wessex
814 Sqn		(reformed)	30.3.73	9.4.76	Culdrose	Sea King
819 Sqn		HMS Hermes	13.7.79	-	(current)	Sea King
824C Flt		Culdrose	11.1.82	26.2.82	Culdrose	Sea King
826C Flt		Culdrose	11.1.82	26.2.82	Culdrose	Sea King
824A Flt		RFA Olmeda	22.2.82	30.3.82	Culdrose	Sea King
826B Flt		Culdrose	25.8.86	24.9.86	Culdrose	Sea King
824 Sqn		Benbecula	1.10.87	8.89	(disbanded)	Sea King

Control
Buildings 50Ft
N

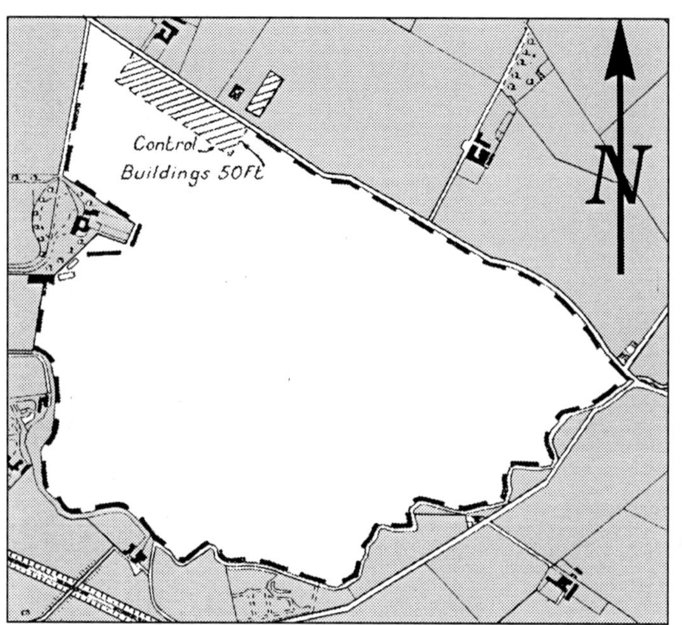

Left: From Air Pilot, 1938, the landing ground at Prestwick.

Below: a confidential sheet, giving the details for Prestwick, Scotland, dated 26 January 1945. The call-sign was for the Control Tower was 'Burton'. Airways being 'Burton Control'

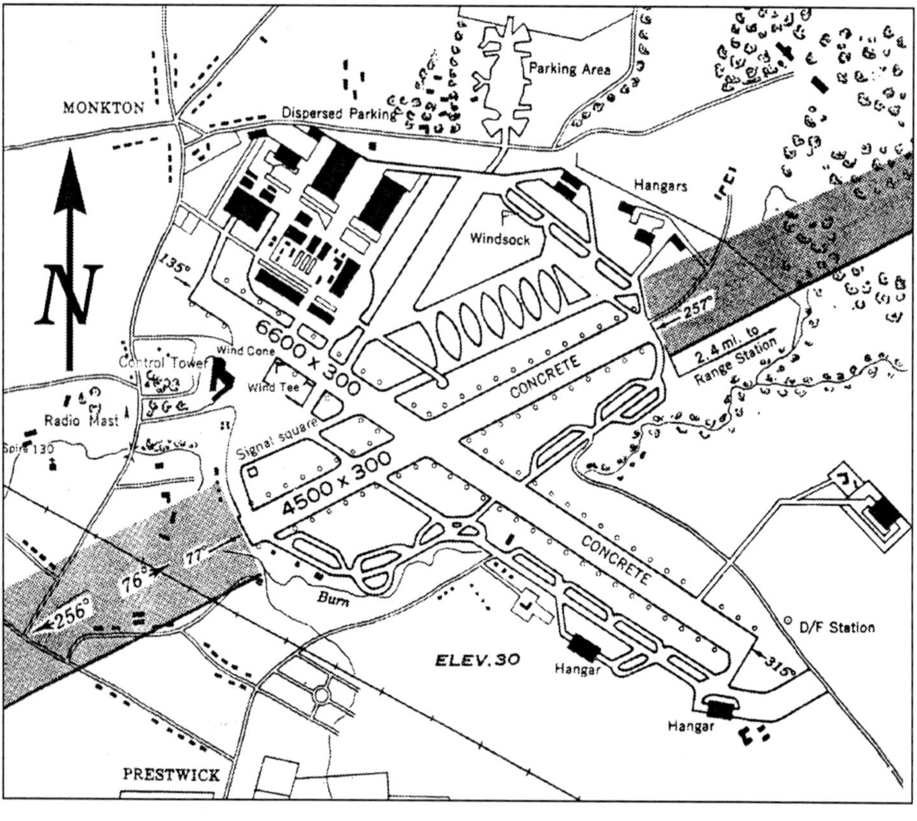

MONKTON
Dispersed Parking
Parking Area
Hangars
Windsock
135°
N
6600 x 300
CONCRETE
257°
2.4 mi. to
Range Station
Control Tower
Wind Cone
Wind Tee
Radio Mast
Spire 130
Signal square
4500 x 300
CONCRETE
77°
76°
256°
Burn
D/F Station
ELEV. 30
Hangar
315°
Hangar
PRESTWICK